FOR ALL ORGANS, PIANO & GUITAR

E-Z PLAY TODAY

THE MUSIC MAN

T0045352

E-Z Play TODAY is designed for you!

- All songs are arranged for use with all major brand organs.

- Special chord notation for SINGLE KEY CHORDS . . . TRIAD CHORDS . . . and STANDARD CHORD POSITIONS.

- The result . . . INSTANT PLAYING ENJOYMENT!

Contents

FRANK
MUSIC CORP.

EXCLUSIVELY DISTRIBUTED BY

HAL•LEONARD®
CORPORATION

7777 W. BLUEMOUND RD. P.O. BOX 13819 MILWAUKEE, WI 53213

Till There Was You

Registration 2
Rhythm: Ballad

By Meredith Willson

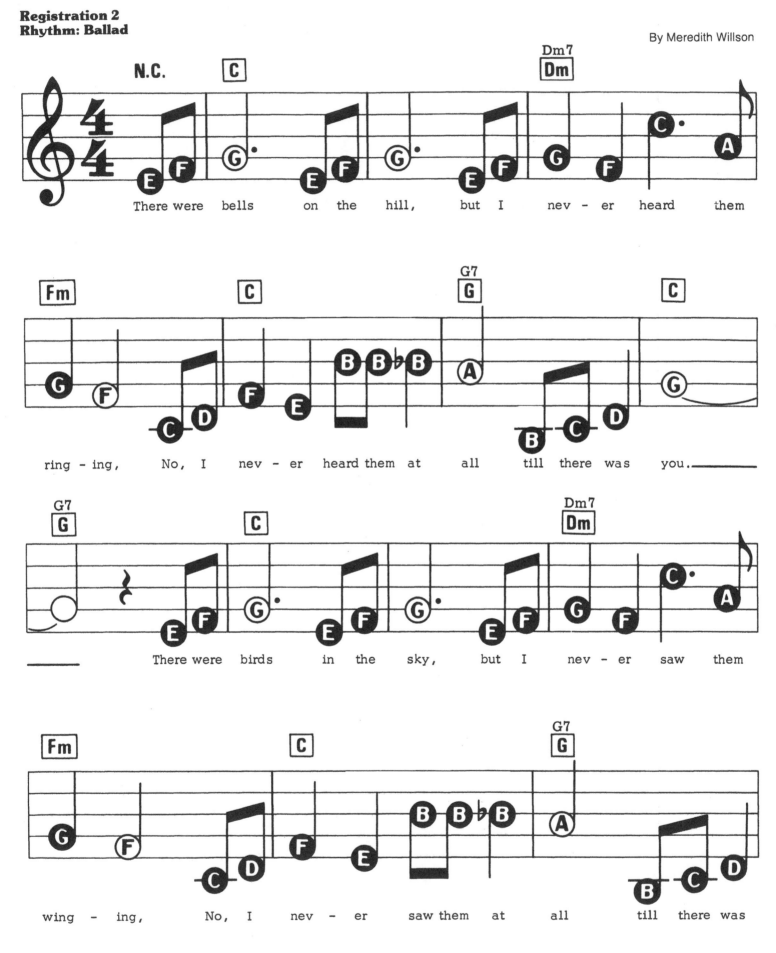

3

Good Night, My Someone

Registration 10
Rhythm: Waltz

By Meredith Willson

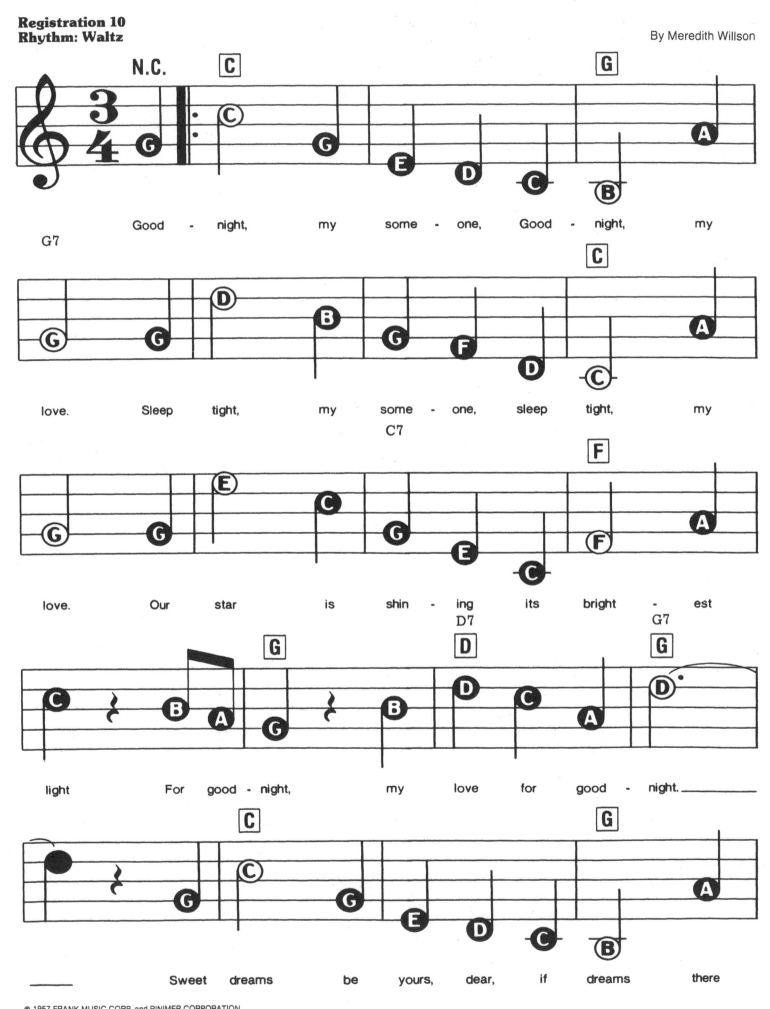

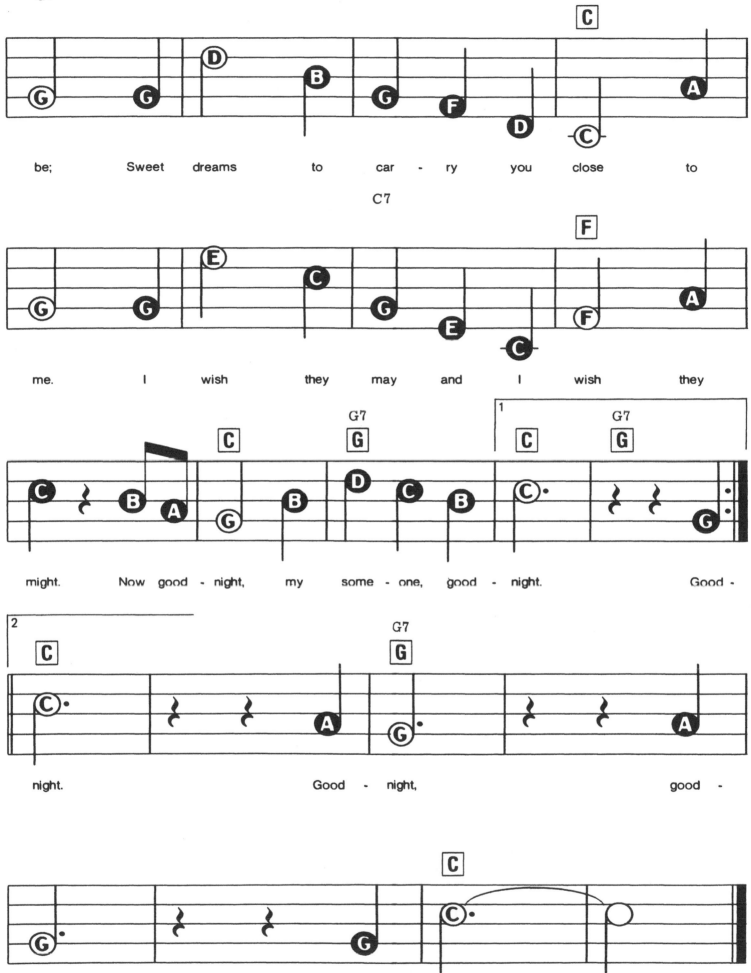

be;   Sweet dreams to car - ry you close to

me.   I wish they may and I wish they

might.   Now good - night, my some - one, good - night.   Good -

night.   Good - night,   good -

night,   good - night._____

Seventy Six Trombones

Registration 5
Rhythm: 6/8 March

By Meredith Willson

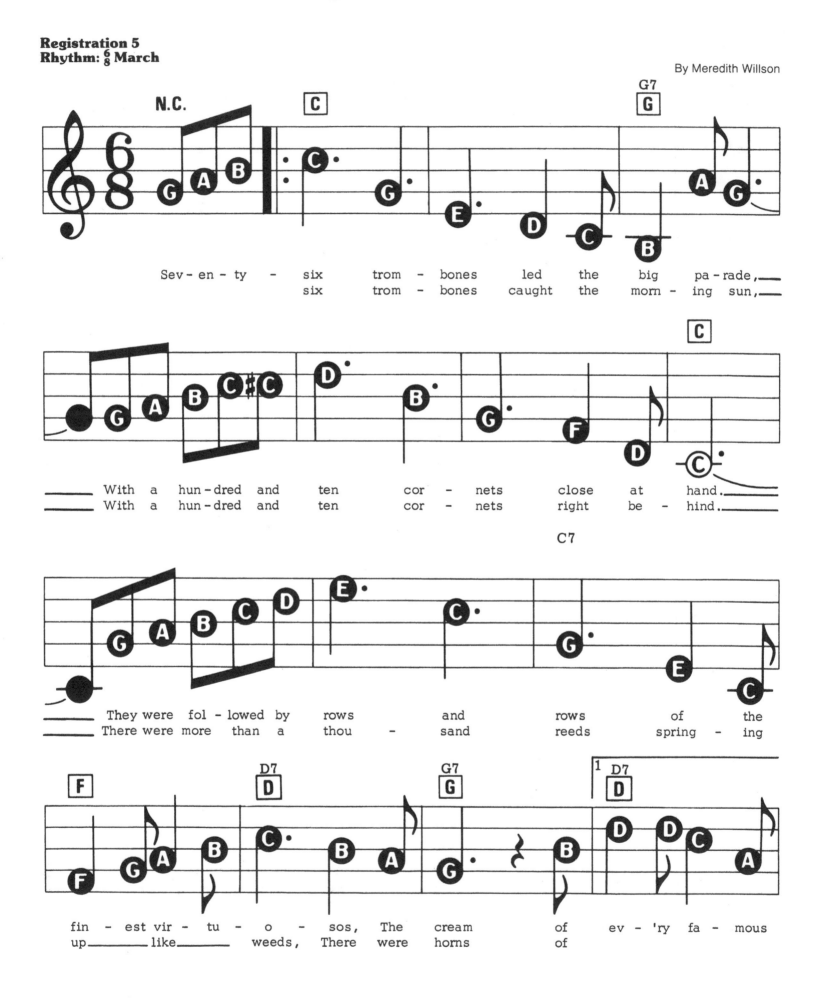

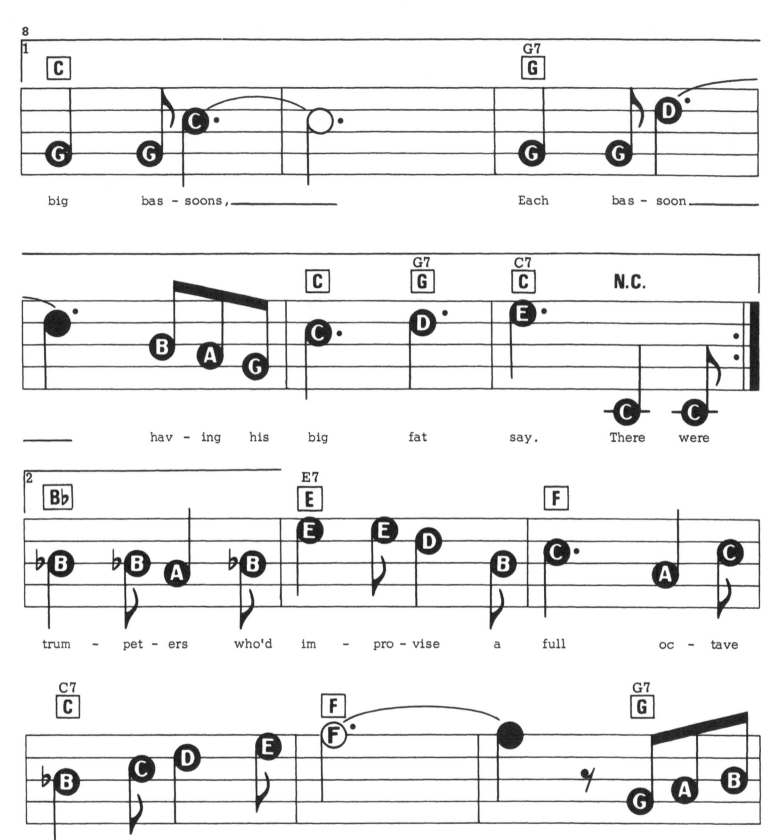

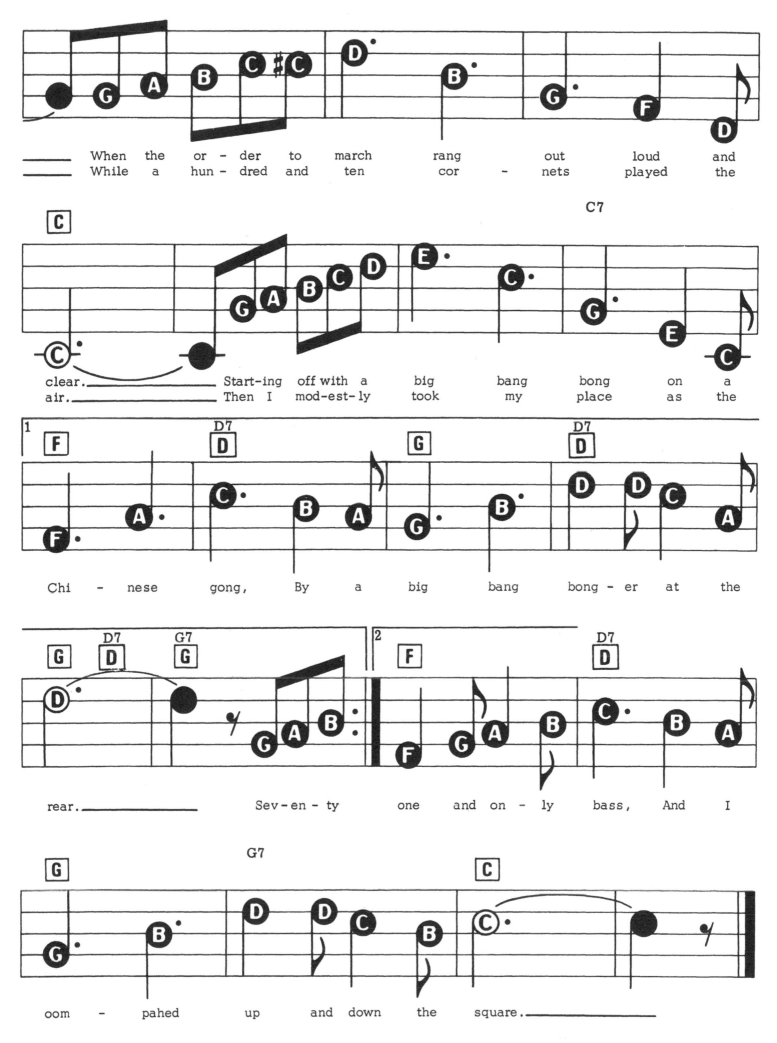

It's You

Registration 3
Rhythm: Swing

By Meredith Willson

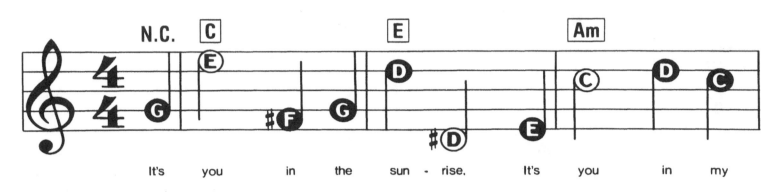

It's you in the sun - rise, It's you in my

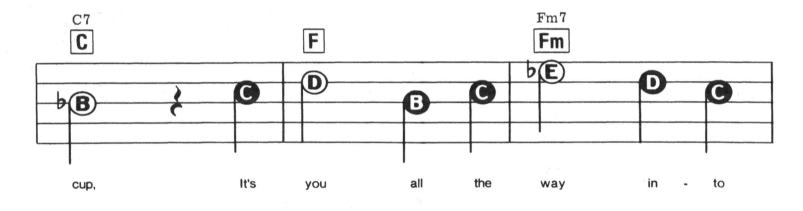

cup, It's you all the way in - to

town. _____ It's your sweet "hel -

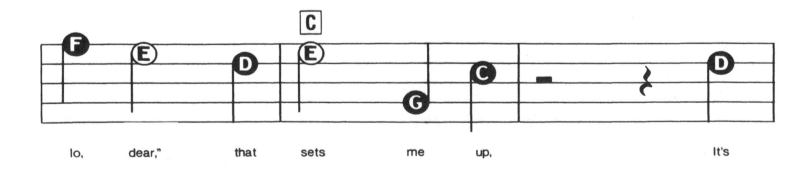

lo, dear," that sets me up, It's

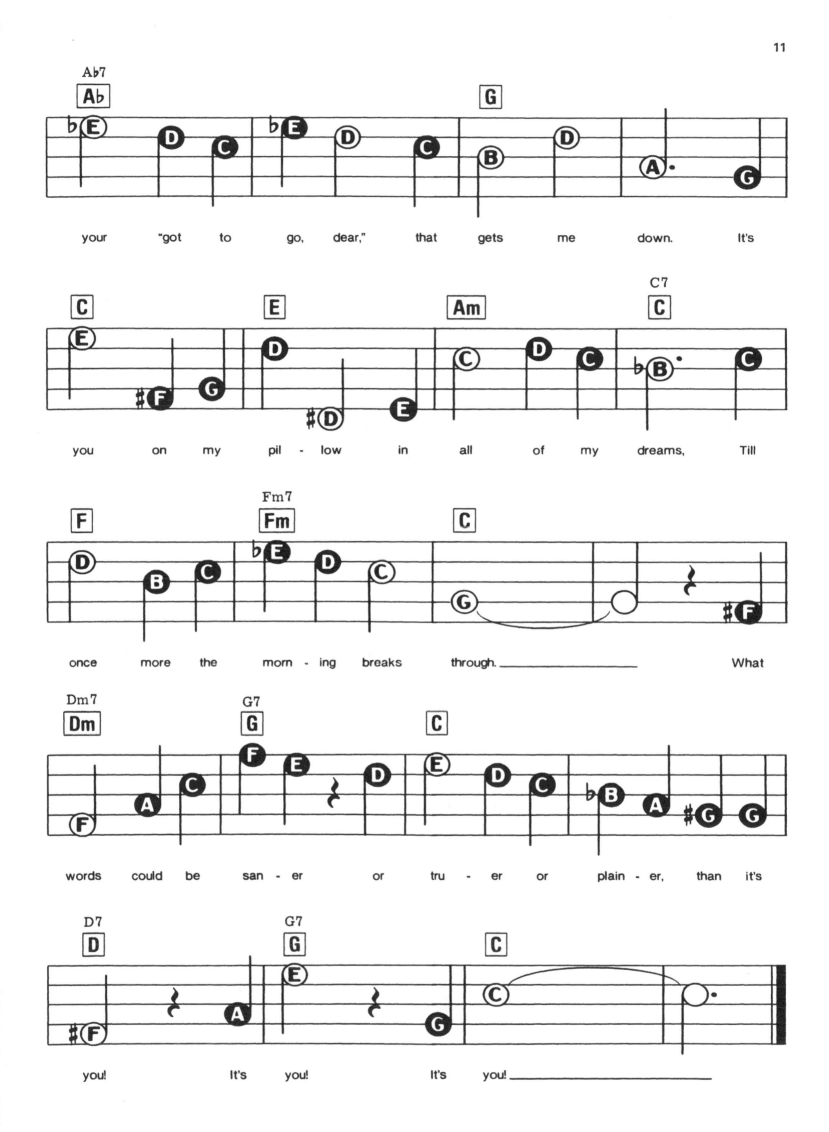

Lida Rose

Registration 9
Rhythm: Ballad

By Meredith Willson

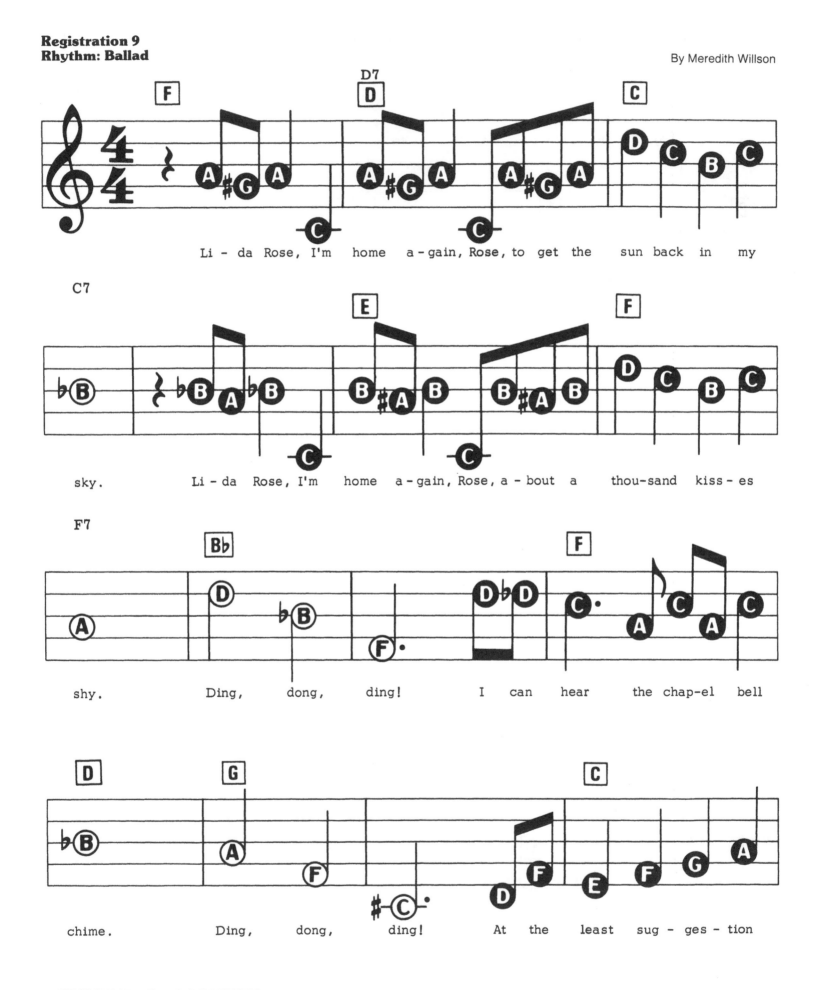

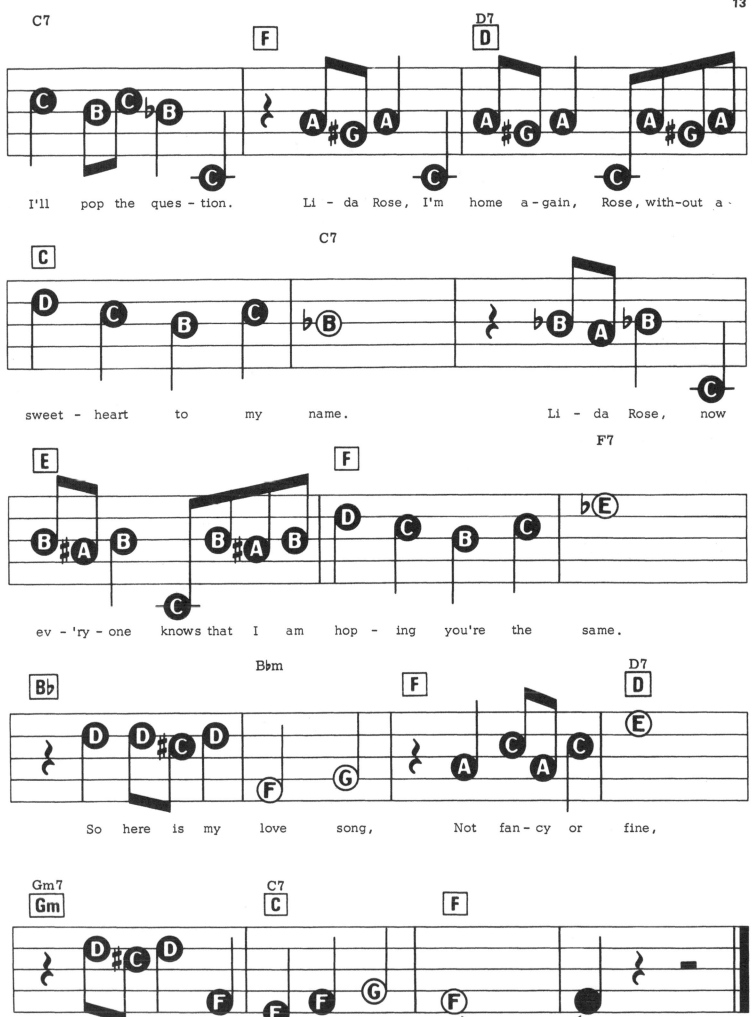

My White Knight

Registration 2
Rhythm: Swing

By Meredith Willson

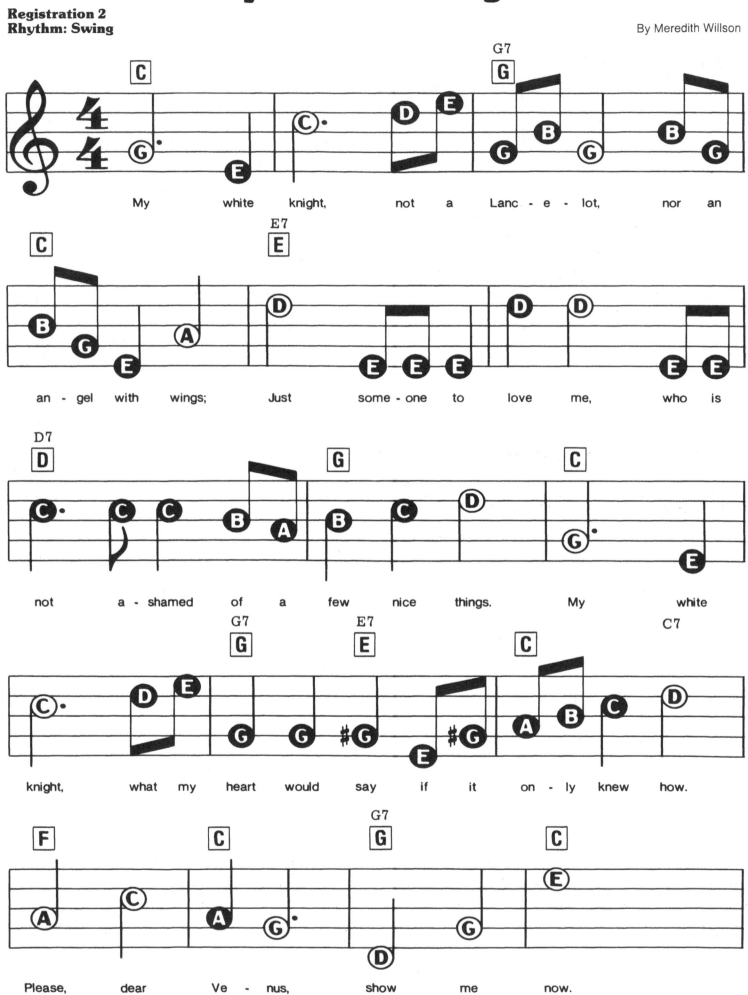

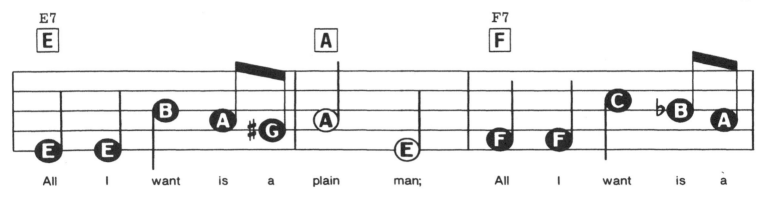

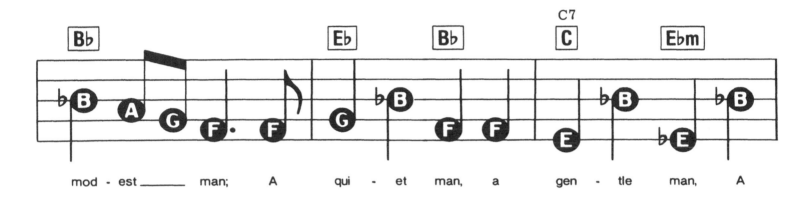

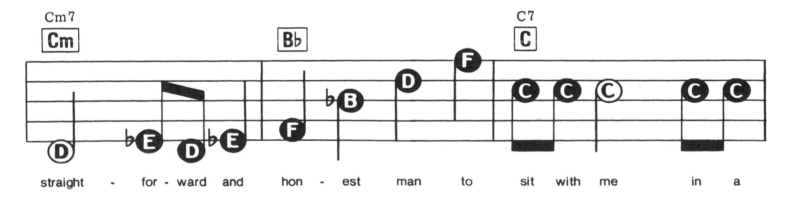

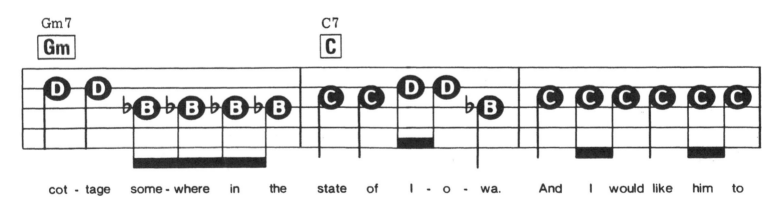

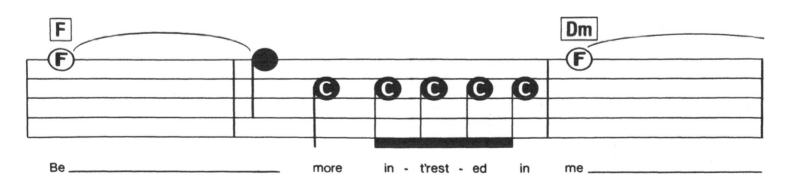

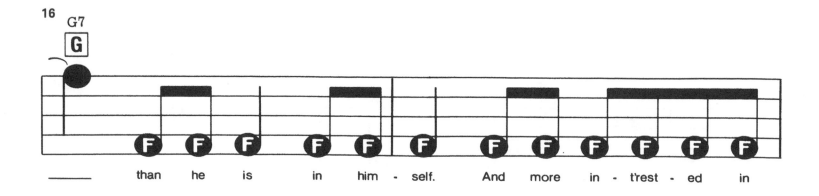

_____ than he is in him - self. And more in - t'rest - ed in

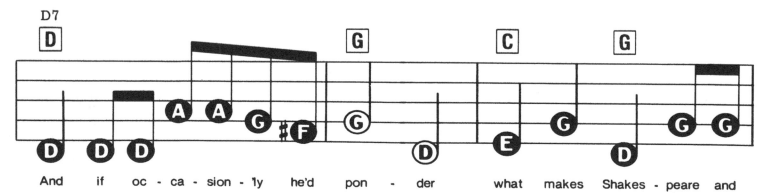

us than in me. _____

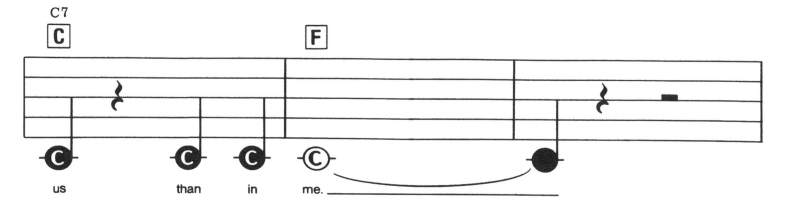

And if oc - ca - sion - 'ly he'd pon - der what makes Shakes - peare and

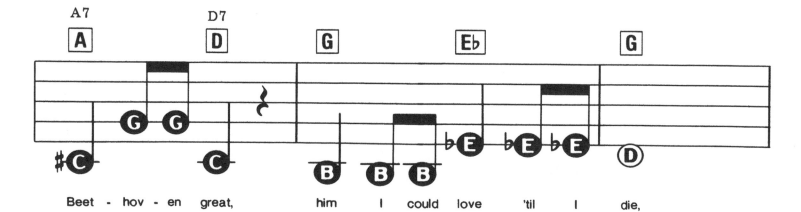

Beet - hov - en great, him I could love 'til I die,

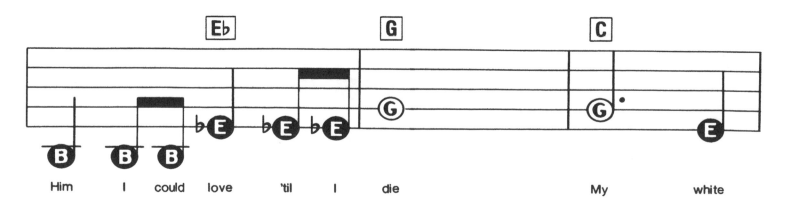

Him I could love 'til I die My white

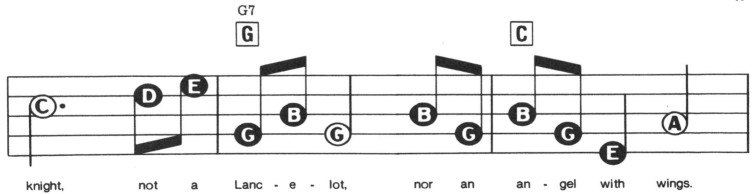

knight, not a Lanc - e - lot, nor an an - gel with wings.

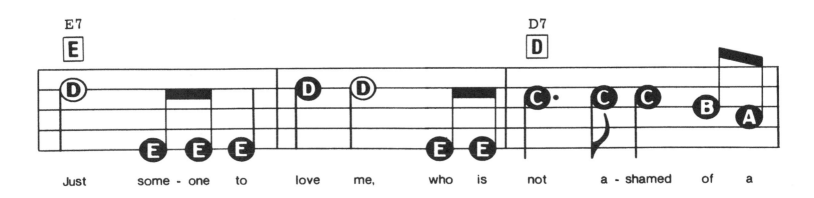

Just some - one to love me, who is not a - shamed of a

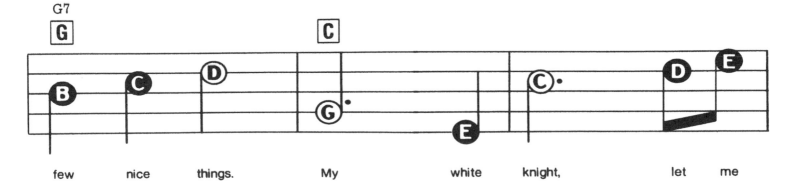

few nice things. My white knight, let me

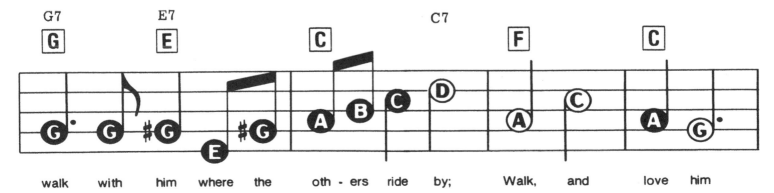

walk with him where the oth - ers ride by; Walk, and love him

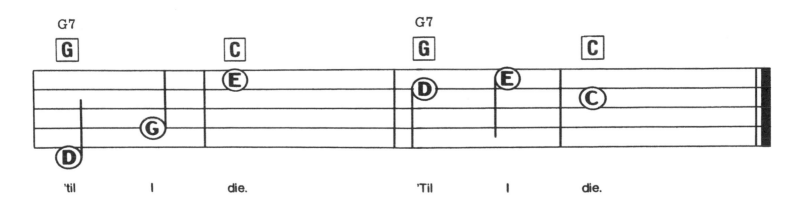

'til I die. 'Til I die.

The Wells Fargo Wagon

Registration 8
Rhythm: March

By Meredith Willson

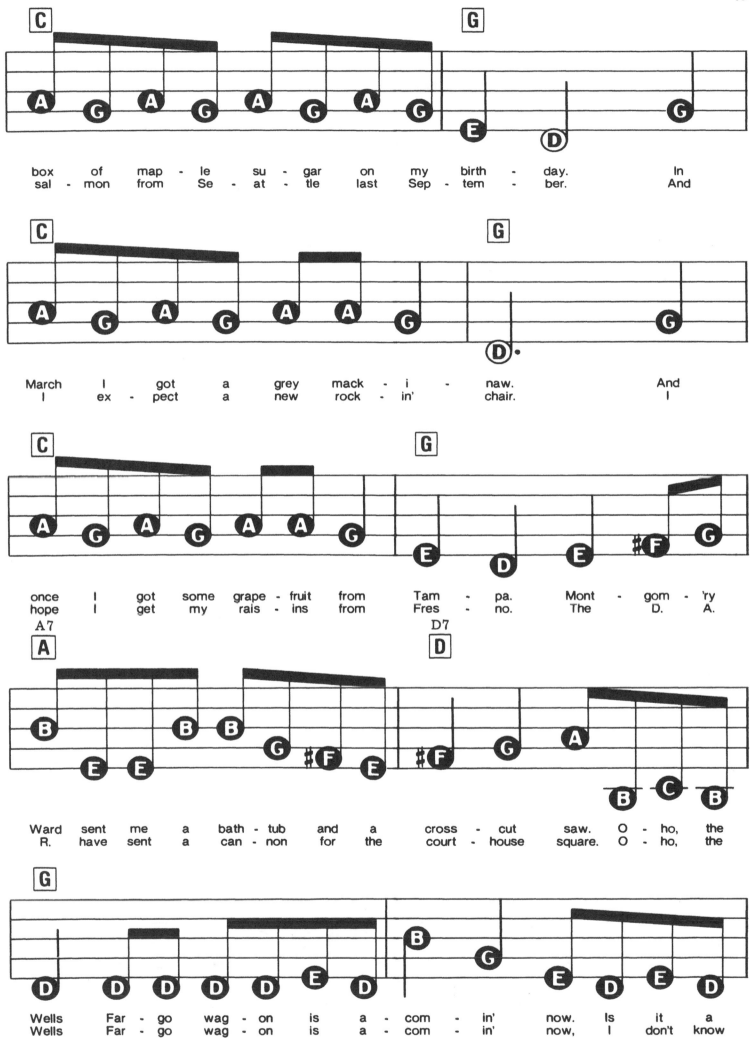

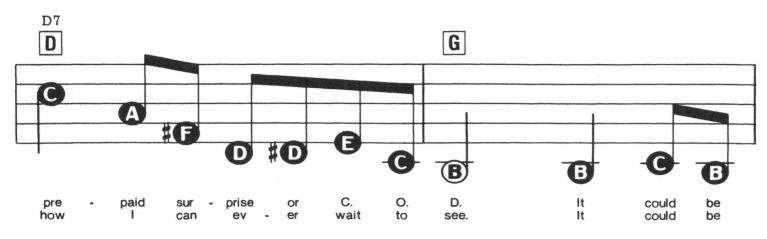

pre - paid sur - prise or C. O. D. It could be
how I can ev - er wait to see. It could be

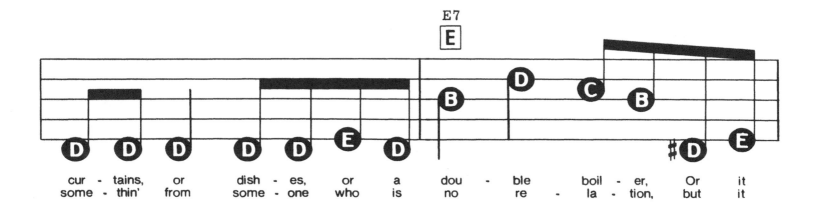

cur - tains, or dish - es, or a dou - ble boil - er, Or it
some - thin' from some - one who is no re - la - tion, but it

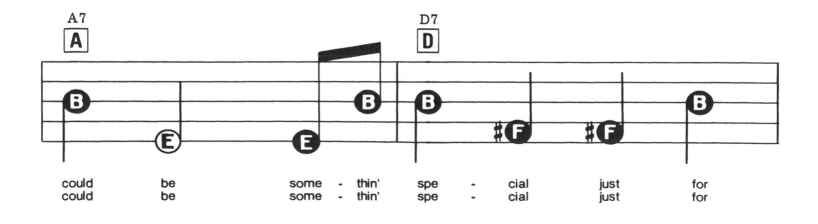

could be some - thin' spe - cial just for
could be some - thin' spe - cial just for

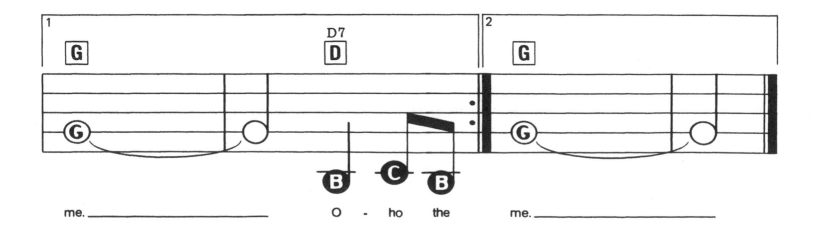

me._____ O - ho the me._____

Gary, Indiana

Registration 1
Rhythm: Swing

By Meredith Willson

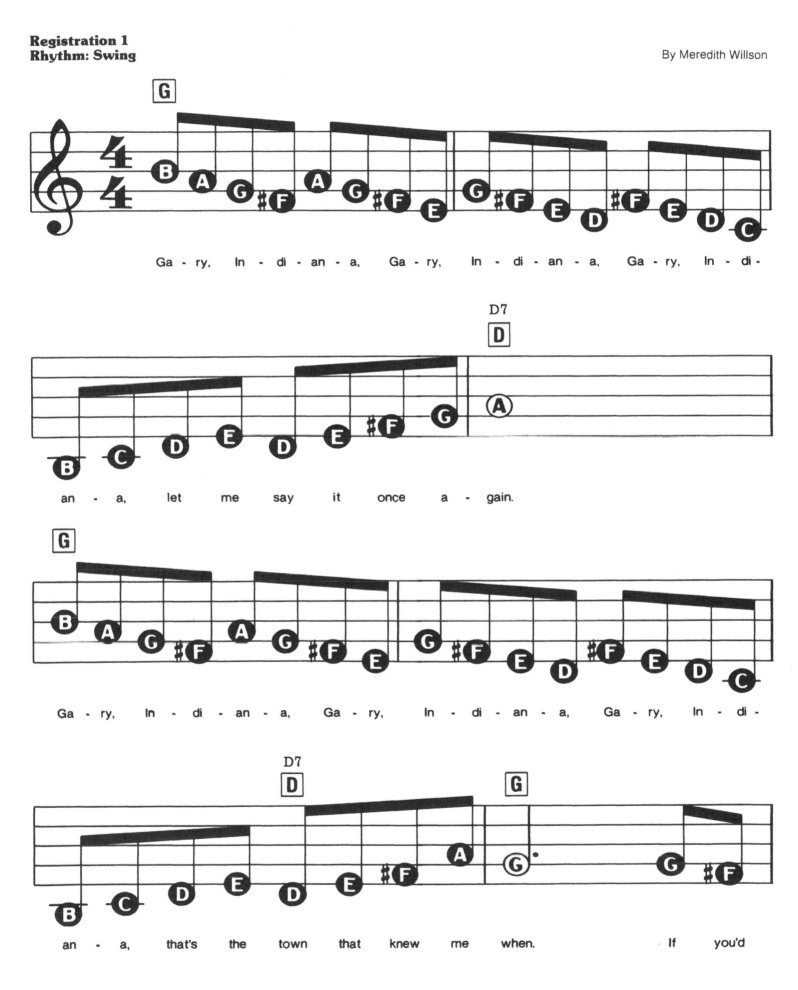

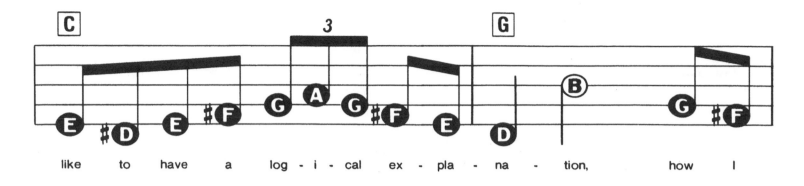

like to have a log - i - cal ex - pla - na - tion, how I

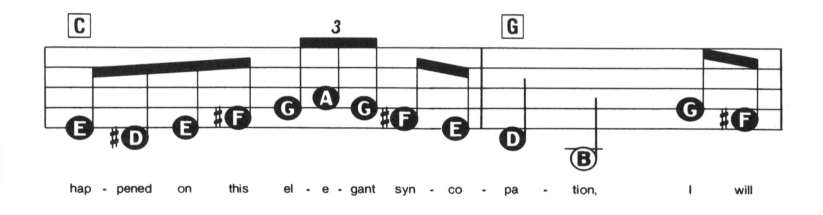

hap - pened on this el - e - gant syn - co - pa - tion, I will

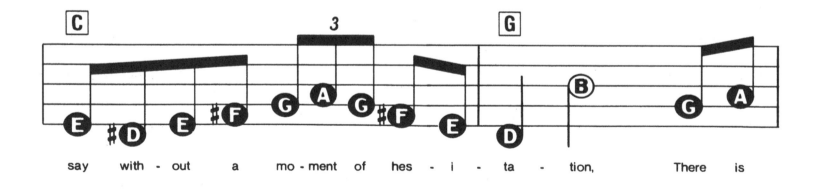

say with - out a mo - ment of hes - i - ta - tion, There is

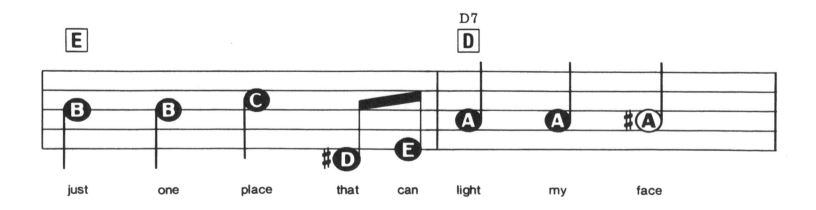

just one place that can light my face

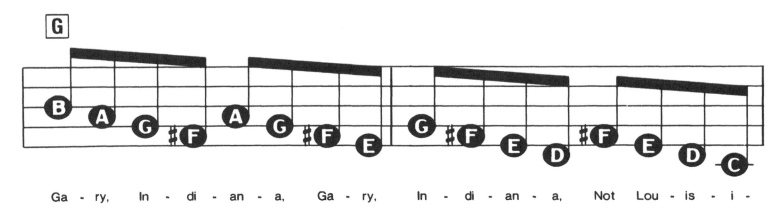

Ga - ry, In - di - an - a, Ga - ry, In - di - an - a, Not Lou - is - i -

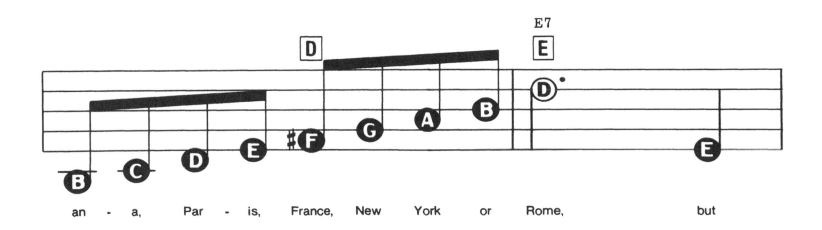

an - a, Par - is, France, New York or Rome, but

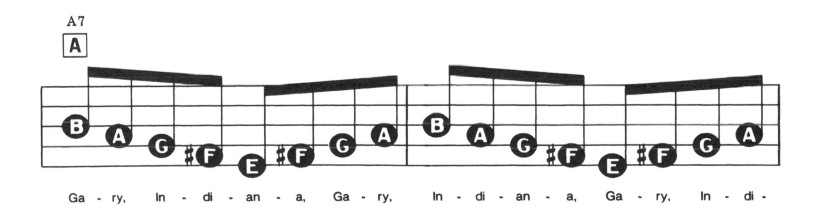

Ga - ry, In - di - an - a, Ga - ry, In - di - an - a, Ga - ry, In - di -

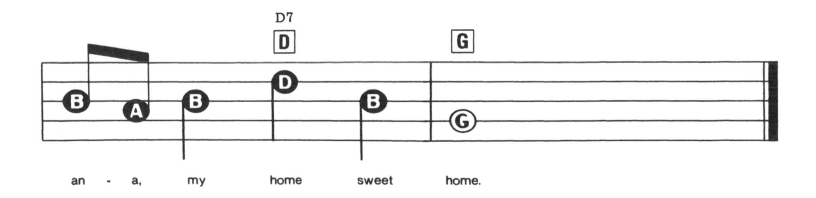

an - a, my home sweet home.

Chord Speller Chart
of Standard Chord Positions

For those who play standard chord positions, all chords used in the E-Z Play TODAY music arrangements are shown here in their most commonly used chord positions. Suggested fingering is also indicated, but feel free to use alternate fingering.

CHORD FAMILY Abbrev.	MAJOR	MINOR (m)	7TH (7)	MINOR 7TH (m7)
C	5 2 1 G-C-E	5 2 1 G-C-Eb	5 3 2 1 G-Bb-C-E	5 3 2 1 G-Bb-C-Eb
Db	5 2 1 Ab-Db-F	5 2 1 Ab-Db-E	5 3 2 1 Ab-B-Db-F	5 3 2 1 Ab-B-Db-E
D	5 3 1 F#-A-D	5 2 1 A-D-F	5 3 2 1 F#-A-C-D	5 3 2 1 A-C-D-F
Eb	5 3 1 G-Bb-Eb	5 3 1 Gb-Bb-Eb	5 3 2 1 G-Bb-Db-Eb	5 3 2 1 Gb-Bb-Db-Eb
E	5 3 1 G#-B-E	5 3 1 G-B-E	5 3 2 1 G#-B-D-E	5 3 2 1 G-B-D-E
F	4 2 1 A-C-F	4 2 1 Ab-C-F	5 3 2 1 A-C-Eb-F	5 3 2 1 Ab-C-Eb-F
F#	4 2 1 F#-A#-C#	4 2 1 F#-A-C#	5 3 2 1 F#-A#-C#-E	5 3 2 1 F#-A-C#-E
G	5 3 1 G-B-D	5 3 1 G-Bb-D	5 3 2 1 G-B-D-F	5 3 2 1 G-Bb-D-F
Ab	4 2 1 Ab-C-Eb	4 2 1 Ab-B-Eb	5 3 2 1 Ab-C-Eb-Gb	5 3 2 1 Ab-B-Eb-Gb
A	4 2 1 A-C#-E	4 2 1 A-C-E	5 4 2 1 G-A-C#-E	5 4 2 1 G-A-C-E
Bb	4 2 1 Bb-D-F	4 2 1 Bb-Db-F	5 4 2 1 Ab-Bb-D-F	5 4 2 1 Ab-Bb-Db-F
B	5 2 1 F#-B-D#	5 2 1 F#-B-D	5 3 2 1 F#-A-B-D#	5 3 2 1 F#-A-B-D